Fourth Position Preparatory Studies

for the cello

by Cassia Harvey

CHP260

©2014 by C. Harvey Publications All Rights Reserved.

www.charveypublications.com - print books
www.learnstrings.com - PDF downloadable books
www.harveystringarrangements.com - chamber music

A String

First Position

Fourth Position

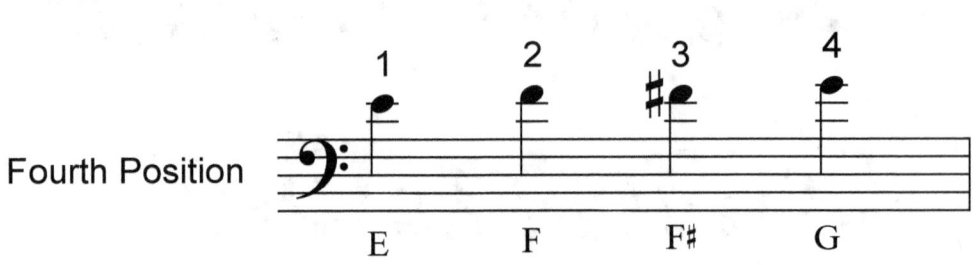

©2014 C. Harvey Publications All Rights Reserved.

Fourth Position Preparatory Studies for Cello 1

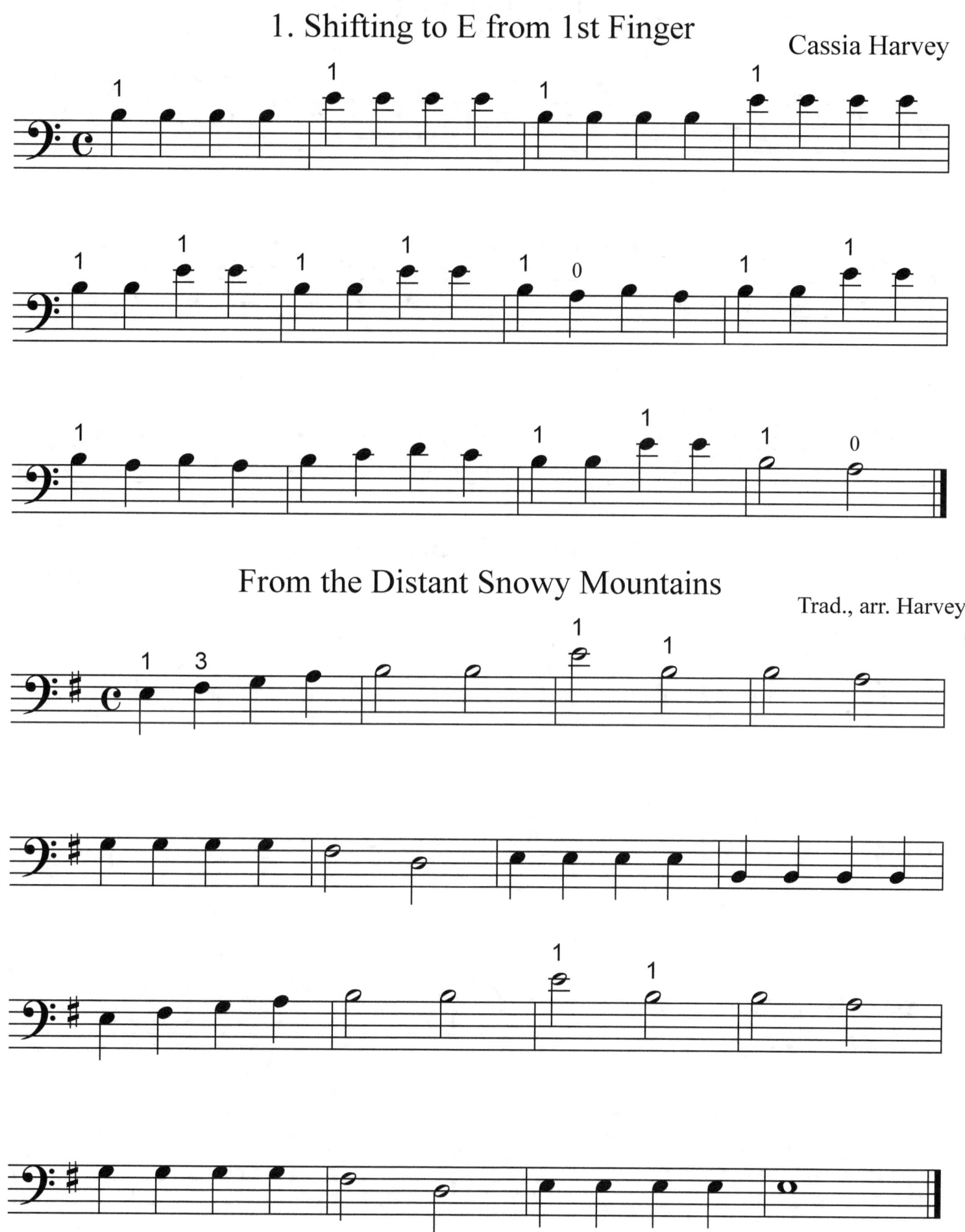

2. Shifting to E in Rhythm

I Heard the Wild Geese Flying

Halvorsen, arr. Harvey

Fourth Position Preparatory Studies for Cello

3. Shifting to E from 1st Finger

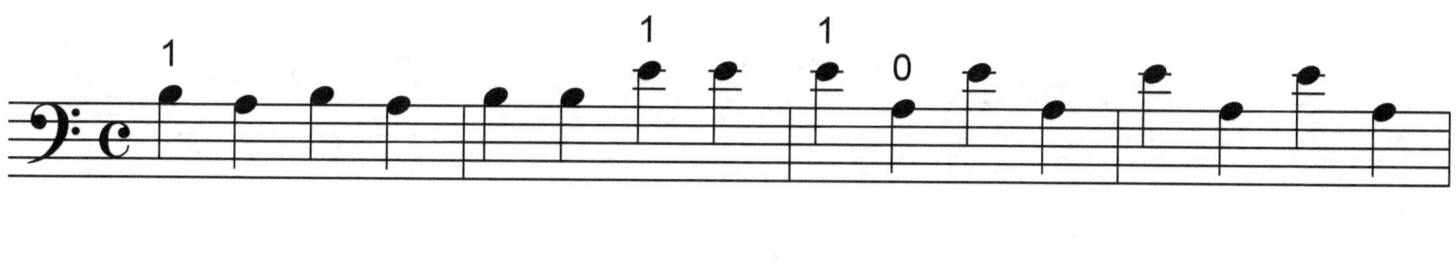

When Night is Falling

Targett, arr. Harvey

©2014 C. Harvey Publications All Rights Reserved.

4. Shifting to E from 2nd Finger

Big Bells Ringing

Trad., arr. Harvey

Fourth Position Preparatory Studies for Cello

5. Shifting to E in Rhythm

Sunrise

Harvey

©2014 C. Harvey Publications All Rights Reserved.

6. Shifting Back from E to 2nd Finger

The Tailor and the Mouse

Trad., arr. Harvey

Fourth Position Preparatory Studies for Cello

7. Shifting to E from 3rd Finger

Scaling the Peaks

Harvey

©2014 C. Harvey Publications All Rights Reserved.

8. Shortnin' Bread

Trad., arr. Harvey

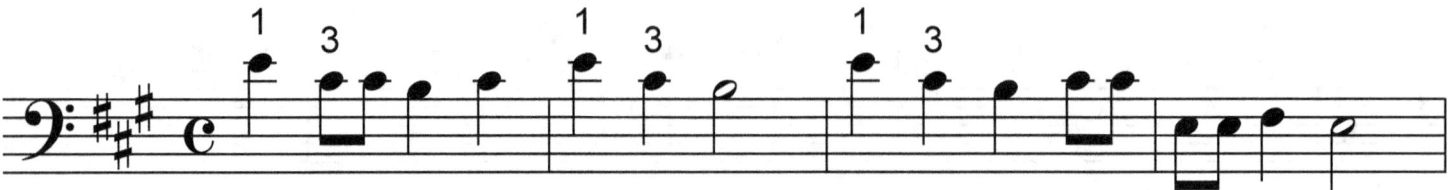

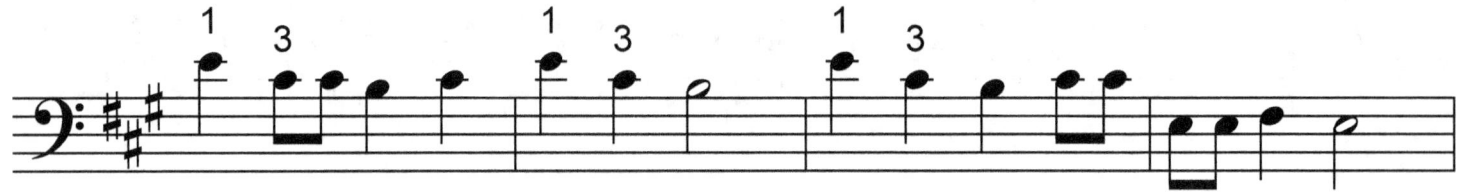

White Dove

Trad., arr. Harvey

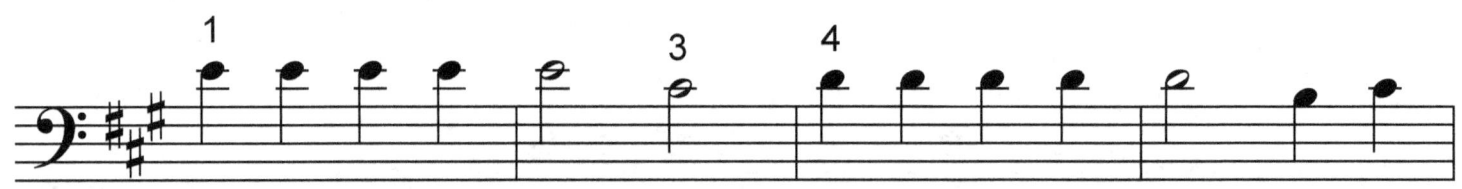

©2014 C. Harvey Publications All Rights Reserved.

9. Shifting to E from 4th Finger

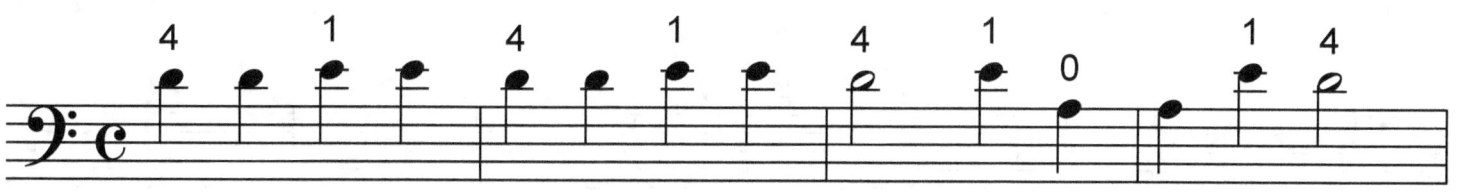

Bartolillo

Trad., arr. Harvey

10. Nous n'irons plus au bois

Trad., arr. Harvey

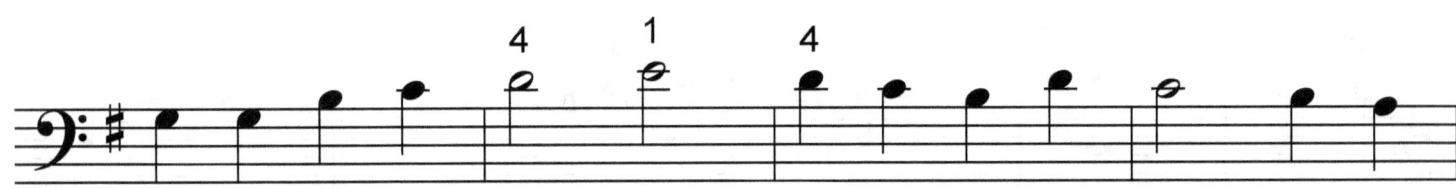
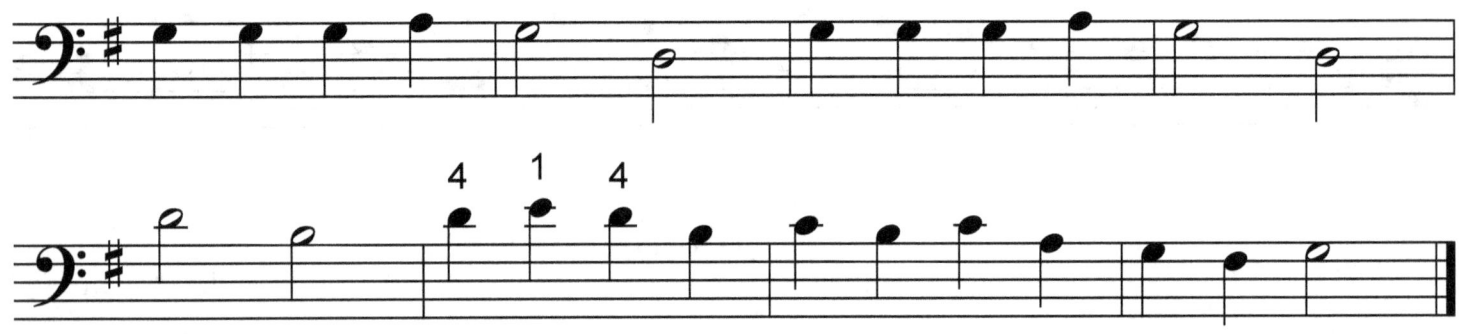

Daffodils

Brockwell, arr. Harvey

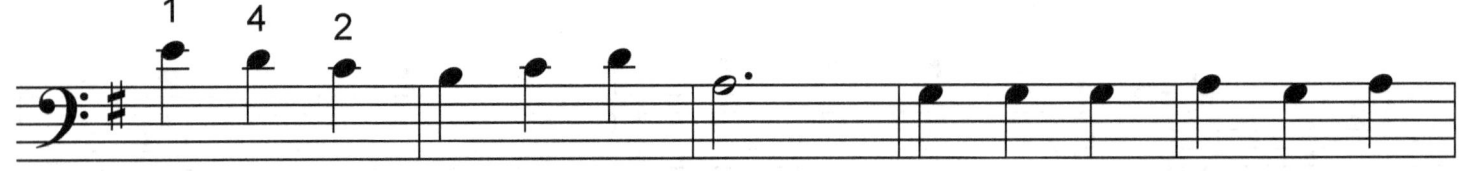

©2014 C. Harvey Publications All Rights Reserved.

Fourth Position Preparatory Studies for Cello

11. Shifting to E

Ah! mon beau Chateau

Trad., arr. Harvey

©2014 C. Harvey Publications All Rights Reserved.

12. Shifting to E from All Fingers

Oh, Susannah
Foster, arr. Harvey

Fourth Position Preparatory Studies for Cello

13. Shifting to 2nd Finger F

Pulsars
Harvey

14. Shifting to F from 2nd Finger

Orbits
Harvey

Fourth Position Preparatory Studies for Cello

15. More Shifting to F

Tadpoles

Forde, arr. Harvey

©2014 C. Harvey Publications All Rights Reserved.

16. Shifting to F from 3rd Finger

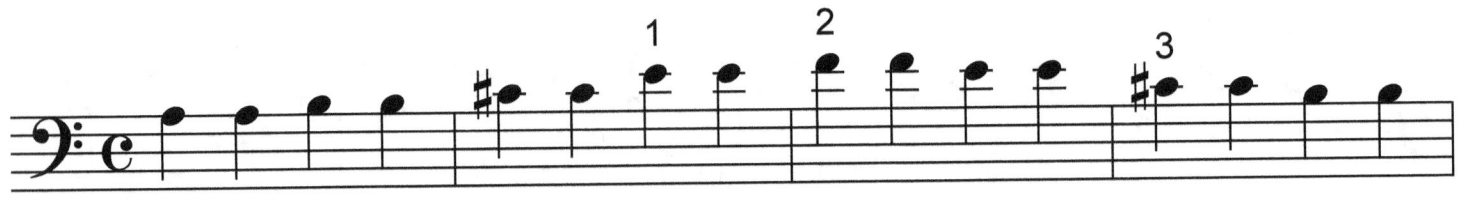

Quasars

Harvey

©2014 C. Harvey Publications All Rights Reserved.

Fourth Position Preparatory Studies for Cello

17. Shifting to F from All Fingers

Promenade
Harvey

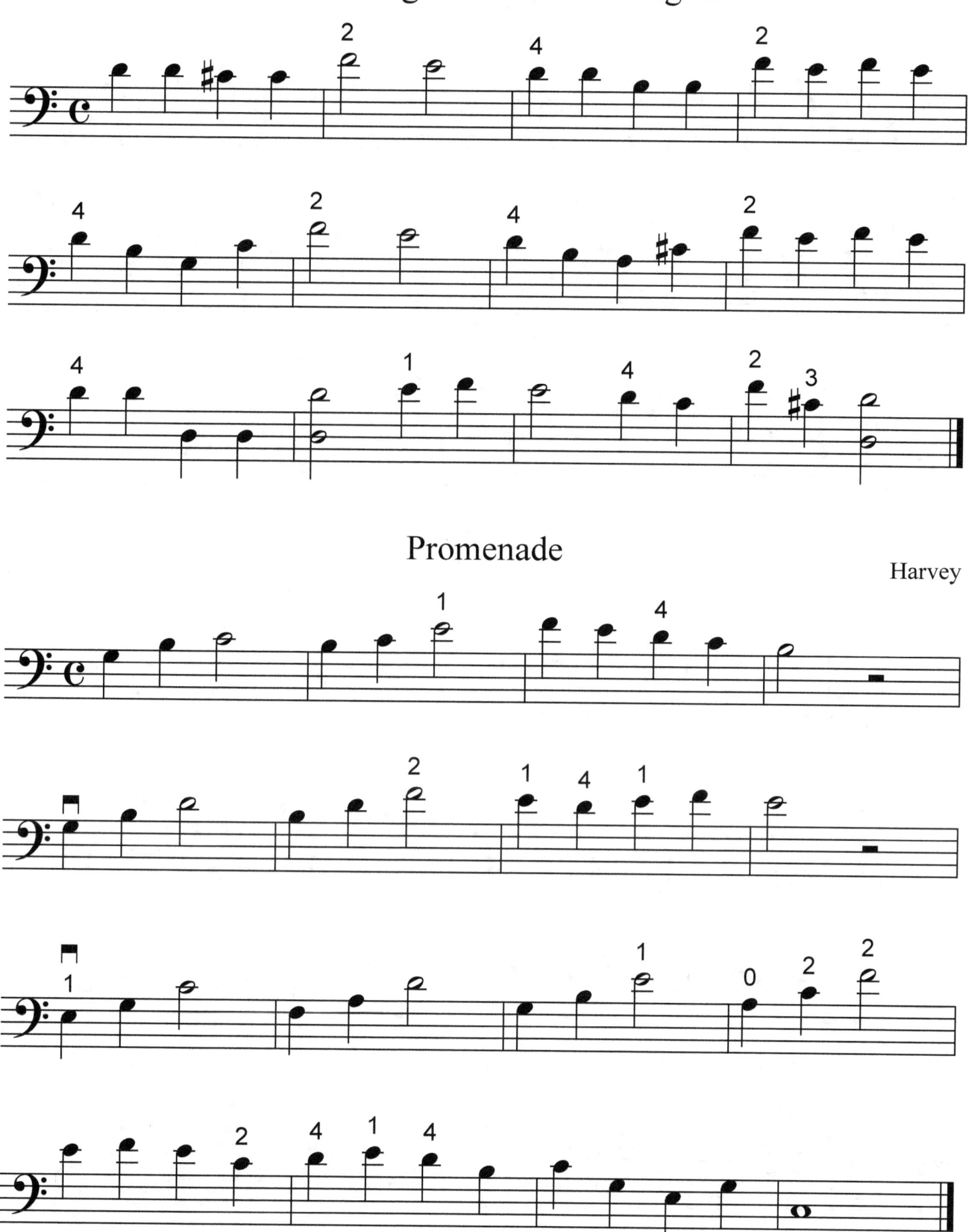

©2014 C. Harvey Publications All Rights Reserved.

18. Shifting to F from 4th Finger

The Pier
Harvey

Fourth Position Preparatory Studies for Cello

19. Shifting to F#

Boutique Fantasque

Trad., arr. Harvey

©2014 C. Harvey Publications All Rights Reserved.

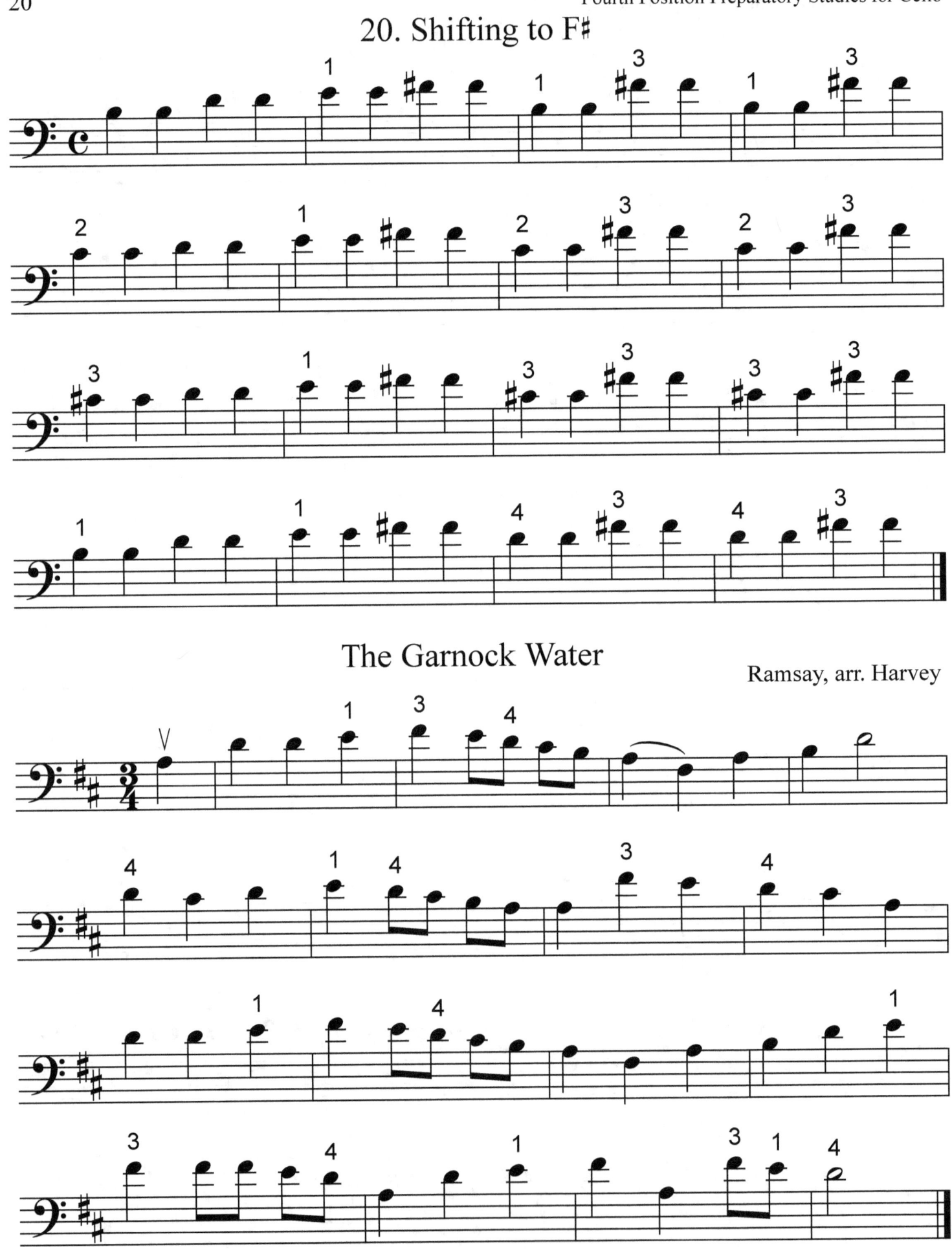

Fourth Position Preparatory Studies for Cello

21. Shifting to F#

The Trent Waltz

Beethoven, arr. Harvey

©2014 C. Harvey Publications All Rights Reserved.

22. Little F# Finger Exercise

Alleluia
Mozart, arr. Harvey

Fourth Position Preparatory Studies for Cello

23. Shifting to F# in Rhythm

The Grass Rustles

Trad., Harvey

©2014 C. Harvey Publications All Rights Reserved.

24. F# and F♮

The White Fish Played

Trad., arr. Harvey

Fourth Position Preparatory Studies for Cello

25. F# Review

Ukrainian Folk Song

Trad., arr. Harvey

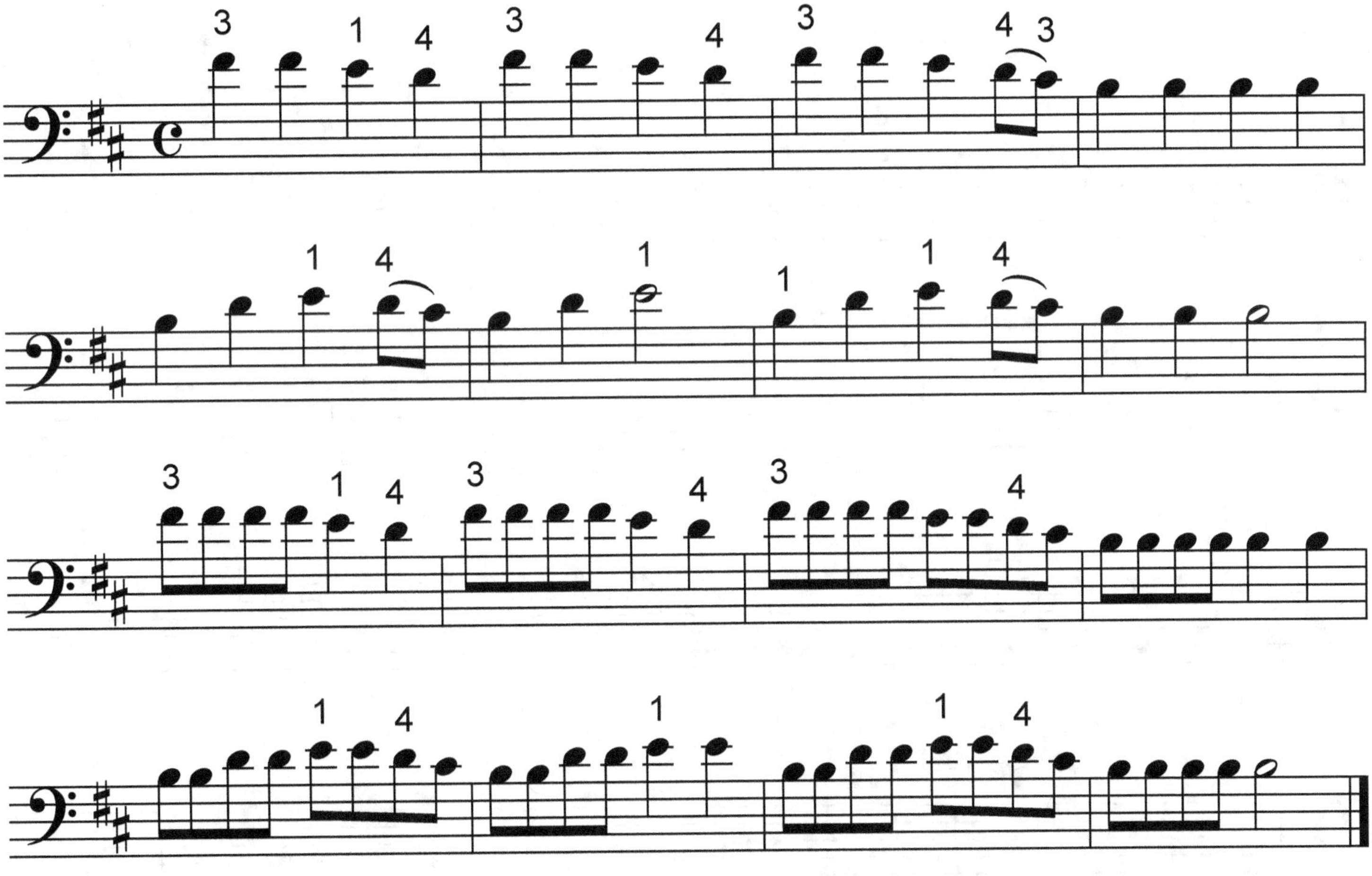

©2014 C. Harvey Publications All Rights Reserved.

Fourth Position Preparatory Studies for Cello

27. Playing 4th Finger G

Oh, in Petrivochka the Night is Too Short

Trad., arr. Harvey

©2014 C. Harvey Publications All Rights Reserved.

28. Shifting to G

Oh Kumko, Borrow Barrels

Trad., arr. Harvey

©2014 C. Harvey Publications All Rights Reserved.

Fourth Position Preparatory Studies for Cello

29. Shifting to F# and G

The Merry Allemande

Bast, arr. Harvey

Fourth Position Preparatory Studies for Cello

31. Using 2nd and 4th Fingers

Valse from 'Jordacki'
Von Weber, arr. Harvey

©2014 C. Harvey Publications All Rights Reserved.

Fourth Position Preparatory Studies for Cello

32. Finger Exercise

Rigaudon
Bast, arr. Harvey

©2014 C. Harvey Publications All Rights Reserved.

Fourth Position Preparatory Studies for Cello

33. Shifting During Open Strings

Devil's Dream
Trad., arr. Harvey

©2014 C. Harvey Publications All Rights Reserved.

Fourth Position Preparatory Studies for Cello

35. Shifting and Finger Exercise

Sonata
Telemann, arr. Harvey

©2014 C. Harvey Publications All Rights Reserved.

36. Shifting Back from Fourth Position

Mon Vieux Wagon

Trad., arr. Harvey

Fourth Position Preparatory Studies for Cello

37. The Hare's Trot

Trad., arr. Harvey

©2014 C. Harvey Publications All Rights Reserved.

38. Alpenklange

Wohlfahrt, arr. Harvey

Fourth Position Preparatory Studies for Cello

39. Valse of the Rich City

Hamilton, arr. Harvey

©2014 C. Harvey Publications All Rights Reserved.

available from **www.charveypublications.com**: CHP272

Flying Fiddle Duets for Two Cellos, Book One

John Ryan's Polka

Trad., arr. Myanna Harvey

©2015 C. Harvey Publications. All Rights Reserved.